Free Public Library
NEW HAVEN, CONN.

DATE DUE

FEB 24 2007
JAN 13 2009

Caspar and his Friends

hans baumann
Caspar and his friends
a collection of puppet plays

illustrated by Richard Lebenson

Translation by Joyce Emerson and foreword by George Speaight

henry z. walck incorporated   new york

© Ensslin & Laiblin KG Verlag Reutlingen, 1965
© English translation, J.M. Dent & Sons Ltd, 1967
All rights reserved
First American edition 1968
Standard Book Number: 8098-2400-0
Library of Congress Catalog Card Number: 68-23883
Printed in the United States of America

No royalty charged for stage performance

Contents

Introducing Caspar   1
A Message from Caspar   9
Caspar and His Best Friend   11
Caspar and Caw-rax   18
Caspar at the Lost and Found Office   29
Caspar and Icicle Mike   36
Caspar and Bob the Robber   44
Caspar and the Green Rabbits   54
Caspar in the Desert   64
Caspar and the Magic Feather   72
Caspar and the Giant Fog   82
Caspar and the Tollgate   94
Notes for Puppeteers   109
A Bibliography of Puppet Books   115

Introducing Caspar

Caspar—or Kasperl, as his name is usually spelled—is as well known to German children as Punch is to us. Punch, under various names, has performed all over Europe and the United States for many centuries. He is the comic hero or clown who turns up in many plays. In Germany, puppet shows have always been popular. About a hundred years ago Kasperl began to develop as a different character from Punch; his birthplace was the busy German port of Hamburg. He lost his hunchback, his nose grew smaller, and he began to resemble the typical workman of that town, wearing a red jacket with yellow trimming, blue pants with yellow stripes, a white collar and a blue peaked cap.

In other German towns his appearance differed slightly, but wherever he turned up he was a happy fellow, full of fun and jokes, sometimes mischievous but with no real harm in him. He now appears in hundreds of different plays—not just in one story as Punch and Judy do. The well-known German writer of children's books, Hans Baumann, has written some more plays for him and these have been translated into English. I hope that many English and American children will put on these plays themselves with their own puppets, and that Caspar will become as loved a friend and playmate for them as he already is for generations of boys and girls in Germany and Austria.

George Speaight

A Message from Caspar

Welcome, children! Glad to meet you. I'm Caspar and this is my Caspar cap. I've brought you ten brand-new, grand new Caspar plays.

They are all in this book. Which one shall we begin with? I don't mind a bit. I just hope you'll like all of them. I'm there in every one, but shall I tell you which is my favorite? Yes? The longest one of course! And which is the longest one? Well, you can easily find that out for yourselves. I'll just say good-by for now—until the first play begins. Then you'll see me again, because it starts with me.

Oh, but first I have a rhyme to tell you. It's important and I nearly forgot! Listen carefully! Caspar's rhyme goes like this:

> You all know Punch and Judy, yes?
> Punch is my cousin. Did you guess?
> Punch does things he shouldn't do,
> But I am good—as good as you.
> Always, everywhere I go,
> Children love a Caspar show!

Well, that's all for now. Let's get started.

Oh, no . . . just one more thing. At the end of this Caspar book there's something else. Not a play. But any of you who are thinking of putting on one or two or three or all ten of these plays ought to read what there is at the end. Unless, of course, you know it already.

Caspar and His Best Friend

Characters

CASPAR BROOM
TOPKNOT LAZY DEVIL

In Caspar's house. Caspar and his friend Topknot in bed, head to toe, under a bedspread. A clock strikes ten.

CASPAR. (*Sitting up.*) Oooh-er-ah! Ten o'clock already! Topknot, I must shake a leg.

TOPKNOT. Why, Caspar? Bed's best.

CASPAR. And who's going to clean? I have to clean before Grandma comes back.

TOPKNOT. Am I your best friend? Or am I not?

CASPAR. You are, Topknot. You are my best friend.

TOPKNOT. Then you aren't going to leave your best friend.

CASPAR. I don't want to . . . but Grandma said . . .

TOPKNOT. (*Interrupting.*) Fiddlesticks!

CASPAR. You shouldn't talk like that about Grandma.

TOPKNOT. I'll talk how I like! And I won't let you get up.

CASPAR. You see how it is, children? I'm dying to get up—but my friend Topknot won't let me.

BROOM. (*Dancing about in the corner.*) Caspar, come and get me!

CASPAR. Who's that? Who said that?

BROOM. Me! Broom! It's high time you picked me up. Or you won't be ready when Grandma comes back. And then you won't get your doughnut!

CASPAR. I'm coming. (*He tries to get up.*)

TOPKNOT. (*Holding him back.*) I won't let you go! I won't! I won't!

CASPAR. You see, Broom! I want to come and get you—but my friend Topknot won't let me. You'd better come to me instead.

BROOM. I can't move unless you come and get me.

TOPKNOT. Ha ha ha! Ha ha ha!

CASPAR. What's so funny?

TOPKNOT. I'm laughing at that broom. It's getting nowhere—and neither are you!

CASPAR. You're a fine friend today! You're not at all like your usual self.

BROOM. I know why—there's something behind it.

CASPAR. What's behind what?

BROOM. Behind your friend's bad mood. Do you know what you have to do? You have to beat him up a little.

CASPAR. Beat him up a little?

BROOM. Right.

CASPAR. Beat up my friend Topknot?

BROOM. Biff him and bash him! Shake him and smash him!

CASPAR. What has he done to deserve that?

BROOM. (*Dancing about.*)

> Biff him and smash him,
> Bash him about!
> Something's got into him.
> You beat it out!

CASPAR. Why do I have to beat it out, Topknot? Why can't you just tell me what's got into you?

TOPKNOT. What's got into me? I'll tell you what's . . . (*He shivers and shakes.*) Ow! Ow! Ow!

CASPAR. What are you yelling like that for?

TOPKNOT. Because . . . Ow!

CASPAR. For goodness' sake, Topknot! Tell me!

TOPKNOT. I can't.

CASPAR. Then you aren't my best friend at all.

TOPKNOT. Fiddledy-fiddlesticks!

CASPAR. Fiddlesticks yourself!

TOPKNOT. Fiddlesticks to you!

CASPAR. And you! (*They begin hitting each other. Caspar rolls his friend Topknot out of bed and shakes him. A little devil pops out.*) Look at that! It's a sort of little devil, isn't it?

TOPKNOT. I can't tell you.

BROOM. But *I* can! It's the lazybones devil, Bones-ebub.

CASPAR. Who's Bones-ebub?

BROOM. One of the five thousand lazy devils who stop people from getting up in the morning.

CASPAR. Is that right, Topknot?

TOPKNOT. Yes, that's right . . .

CASPAR. Then why didn't you tell me right away?

TOPKNOT. Because he kept pinching and prodding me when I wanted to tell you. And when I wanted to let you get up, he kept pinching and prodding me too.

CASPAR. What a fresh little devil! I'm going to give you a crack on your fresh little horns!

LAZY DEVIL. Yah-boo! Can't catch me! Can't catch me!

CASPAR. Yes, I can! (*He tries to catch the little devil, who whizzes past him, back and forth.*)

LAZY DEVIL. Can't catch me! Can't catch me! And can't get rid of me either!

BROOM. (*Dancing excitedly.*) Come and get me, Caspar! He fears me like fire and ice!

CASPAR. (*Picking up the broom and chasing the little devil with it.*) Yes, this is the way! (*At last he hits the lazy devil who flies off in a high arc.*)

TOPKNOT. Well done, Caspar! Well done, Broom!

CASPAR. So you're pleased now! Before you didn't want to let go of me.

TOPKNOT. It was only because he was pinching and prodding me. Now it's all over.

CASPAR. So now I can get on with the sweeping and cleaning, so that everything's spick-and-span before Grandma comes back.

TOPKNOT. Yes, sweep and clean now, and then Grandma will let you sleep late tomorrow.

CASPAR. And my friend Topknot, too, I suppose!

TOPKNOT. Your best of all friends!

BROOM. So long as the lazy devil doesn't creep back and pinch and prod you again.

CASPAR. I'll tell you what . . . we'll put the broom by the bed. He fears the broom like fire and ice.

BROOM. (*Dancing happily.*) Like fire and ice! Like fire and ice!

CASPAR. Did you hear that, children?

CHILDREN. Yes!

CASPAR. If you have a friend like Topknot, give him my love. But tell him to watch out that Bones-ebub, the lazy devil, doesn't get him too. Good-by for now, children.

Caspar and Caw-rax

Characters

CASPAR   **MR. JONES**
GRANDMA   **CAW-RAX**

Outside Caspar's house.

GRANDMA. Now, then, Caspar! Off to school! Mr. Jones, the teacher, is going by on his way there. Where are you, Caspar? I just saw you in there.

MR. JONES. Good morning, Grandma.

GRANDMA. Good morning, Teacher.

MR. JONES. Has Caspar left for school?

GRANDMA. (*Looking around the house.*) Er . . . yes, I think so.

MR. JONES. He's always late, and there's nothing I can do with him. He always has some excuse or other.

GRANDMA. What does he say?

MR. JONES. One day he says, "I'm sorry I'm late, Teacher, but I had to mail a letter for my Grandma." Another day he says, "I'm sorry I'm late, Teacher, but I had to get some pills from the drugstore for my Grandma." Just excuses, of course.

GRANDMA. Whatever makes him say such things?

MR. JONES. *Who*ever makes him say such things, you mean. It's his friend who lives in the park.

GRANDMA. He has a friend living in the park?

MR. JONES. Yes. Thingummybob . . . he's pitch black. You know—Thing-ummyjig.

GRANDMA. A waiter?

MR. JONES. No, not a waiter. What's-his-name—who hops about, hopping here and hopping there, and croaking ". . . caw-rax!"

GRANDMA. Oh, I see—you mean he's a raven.

MR. JONES. Yes, that's right, the raven Caw-rax, the cleverest raven that ever lived in a park.

GRANDMA. How do you know about this?

MR. JONES. I was a little late myself yesterday, and I saw Caspar playing with his friend Caw-rax. And then I heard Caw-rax invent an excuse for him.

GRANDMA. And what did you do then?

MR. JONES. I thought to myself: this is a matter for Caspar's Grandma. She'll know how to deal with the problem. So there you are—good luck with Caw-rax! And good-by until tomorrow.

GRANDMA. Good-by, Mr. Jones. Now I'd better see if that rascal is still inside, late for school as usual!

In Caspar's house. A closet (the front only is enough) is on the right; a door in the center; a window on the left. Closet, door and window can all be opened.

GRANDMA. (*Enters, looking to right and left.*) It's always the same when it's time for school—no Caspar to be seen . . . (*Opens the door.*) Not in his room! (*Opens the window.*) Not out back! Where *can* that rascal be! (*The sound of a sneeze and a dull thud.*) Did you hear what I heard, children?

CHILDREN. Yes!

GRANDMA. Was it a pistol shot?

CHILDREN. No!

GRANDMA. A thunderclap?

CHILDREN. No!

GRANDMA. No. I know what it was. A sneeze—Caspar's sneeze. And what bumped against the closet door? Caspar's head. (*She bangs energetically on the closet door.*) Come out of the closet at once!

CASPAR. I'm not in the closet.

GRANDMA. But I can hear you in the closet.

CASPAR. That's just my voice in the closet.

GRANDMA. And what about your nose? Your nose sneezed in the closet.

CASPAR. Grandma dear, please block up the closet keyhole . . . it's so drafty for a sneezy nose.

GRANDMA. Of course, dear sneezy nose. (*Aside to the children.*) I'll teach him. It's going to get much draftier before long! (*Opens the door.*) Let's open the window, too! (*Opens it.*) Now that's a lovely draft. That'll soon get him out.

CASPAR. Atishoo! Atishoo! (*The closet door flies open and Caspar tumbles out. He has his school bag.*)

GRANDMA. Good morning, little sneezy nose! So you *were* there after all.

CASPAR. What a terrible draft!

GRANDMA. Up you go, little sneezy nose!

CASPAR. Why are you calling me sneezy nose?

GRANDMA. You told me there was only a sneezy nose in the closet. You said you weren't there yourself—and you wouldn't tell a fib, would you?

CASPAR. Er . . . no. But . . .

GRANDMA. No buts! Off you go to school.

CASPAR. Isn't there a letter to be mailed?

GRANDMA. No, thank you.

CASPAR. Don't you want any pills from the drugstore?

GRANDMA. No, thank you.

CASPAR. Shall I run around to Mrs. Jolly to say you can't see her today?

GRANDMA. No, thank you. It's time you left for school, or you'll be late.

CASPAR. Yes, I must hurry. (*Exit.*)

GRANDMA. I'm going to hurry too . . . into the park. It's lucky I know a short cut. But what's this? Caspar's doughnut. He's forgotten to take it with him . . . the rascal!

In the park. Three bushes.

CAW-RAX. I've been waiting for Caspar such a long time.

CASPAR. I'm sorry, Caw-rax. I got delayed. First it was the teacher.

CAW-RAX. What! The teacher delayed you?

CASPAR. He was talking to my Grandma and I couldn't disturb them.

CAW-RAX. No, of course not.

CASPAR. And then my Grandma delayed me.

CAW-RAX. She delayed you too?

CASPAR. Yes. She wanted to play hide-and-seek.

CAW-RAX. She hid first?

CASPAR. No, I hid first, and Grandma found me in the closet.

CAW-RAX. Well I never! That's a wonderful excuse! "I'm sorry to be late, Teacher, but I had to play a game of hide-and-seek with my Grandma."

CASPAR. That's the best excuse you've thought up, Caw-rax!

CAW-RAX. And now you'll play with me?

CASPAR. What shall we play?

CAW-RAX. Hide-and-seek, of course!

CASPAR. All right . . . but only once. Or I'll be *too* late.

CAW-RAX. You hide, I'll seek.

CASPAR. It's cheating to peek. (*He hides behind the bush on the right.*)

CAW-RAX. I'll count to ten . . . (*Putting his head down. Pecking with his beak.*) One, two, three, four, five, six, seven, eight, nine, ten! (*He looks behind the bush on the left.*)

CASPAR. (*Leaping onto the place where Caw-rax was standing and banging three times with his hand on the ground.*) One, two, three . . . couldn't find me!

CAW-RAX. Now I'll hide . . .

CASPAR. No, I must really go to school now!

CAW-RAX. Then I'll come part of the way with you. But I'm rather hungry.

CASPAR. Oh, how silly I am! I've forgotten my doughnut—or lost it.

CAW-RAX. I'll look for it, and if I find it I'll keep it for you. (*Exeunt.*)

GRANDMA. (*Coming out from behind the bush in the center.*) That's how I'll catch him. With the doughnut. Shall I put it here, children?

CHILDREN. Yes.

GRANDMA. Children, tell me this: is it right to be late for school?

CHILDREN. No.

GRANDMA. Or to invent excuses?

CHILDREN. No.

GRANDMA. No! And that's why I must teach Caw-rax a lesson. You won't tell on me, will you, children?

CHILDREN. No.

GRANDMA. Here comes the raven—and I can see he's raven-ous! (*Hides.*)

CAW-RAX. Caw-rax, caw-rax, I'm dying of hunger. I hope I find that doughnut. (*Hops closer.*) How did that get there? Ooh! It smells good! Oooh! I bet it tastes good, too. (*He begins to peck at the wrapped doughnut.*) I'll soon get outside this . . . one, two . . .

GRANDMA. (*Creeping up behind and seizing him.*) Three!

CAW-RAX. (*Screaming loudly.*) Caw-rax! Caw-rax! Caw-rax!

GRANDMA. Now just you be quiet! You can talk all you want when we get home—when your friend Caspar comes back from school. But first I'm going to put you in a beautiful cage. (*Exit with Caw-rax.*)

CAW-RAX. (*Shrieking.*) Caw-rax! Caw-rax! Caw-rax!

> In Caspar's house. Caw-rax sitting in a cage on a couple of rods fastened onto the stage.

CAW-RAX. Caw-rax! Caw-rax! Caw-rax!

GRANDMA. What a nice quiet little bird you are!

CAW-RAX. I haven't done anything. I was just playing with Caspar.

GRANDMA. And making him late for school! And thinking up excuses for him!

CAW-RAX. Caspar's coming! He'll be upset when he sees me here.

GRANDMA. He isn't going to see you! I'm going to cover you up. (*She does so.*) And if you're not as quiet as a mouse, I'll never let you out of your cage. Are you going to be quiet? Really, really quiet?

CAW-RAX. Yes, yes, I am!

CASPAR. (*Enters.*) Grandma, I'm starving!

GRANDMA. Didn't you eat your doughnut?

CASPAR. Er . . . I shared it with a friend.

GRANDMA. What friend was that?

CASPAR. You'll never guess, Grandma . . . (*Noticing the covered cage*) What's under that cover?

GRANDMA. You'll never guess, Caspar. But try!

CASPAR. Is it . . . alive or dead?

GRANDMA. Very much alive.

CASPAR. Is it . . . black or white?

GRANDMA. Black as soot.

CASPAR. Can it talk?

GRANDMA. Yes! It chatters like . . . like a boy who's always late for school and who thinks up all sorts of excuses.

CASPAR. It must be my friend Caw-rax!

GRANDMA. (*Pulling off the cover.*) Right!

CASPAR. I guessed right!

GRANDMA. Yes. And now you have to *do* right . . . by your friend Caw-rax.

CASPAR. What do I have to do?

GRANDMA. You have to promise that you won't be late for school again.

CASPAR. But Caw-rax likes playing with me so much.

GRANDMA. Of course . . . but how about playing *after* school?

CASPAR. I'll promise anything if only you'll let him out.

GRANDMA. (*Opening the cage.*) Out you come, Caw-rax! (*Caw-rax hops out and Grandma peers inside the cage.*) What happened to that doughnut?

CAW-RAX. Caw-rax ate it!

CASPAR. Without saving a bit for me?

CAW-RAX. You're going to have something much, much nicer.

CASPAR. What am I going to have, Grandma dear? Some potato chips?

GRANDMA. No, something nicer than that.

CASPAR. A cookie?

GRANDMA. Nicer even than a cookie. Hamburger!

CASPAR. Hooray! Children, I'm going to dance for joy with my Grandma. You'd like that, wouldn't you, Grandma?

GRANDMA. Of course I would! A little exercise will make the hamburger taste even better.

CAW-RAX. (*Croaking.*) Off we go! (*He sings in a croaking voice "Here we go round the mulberry bush!" or some other cheerful song. Grandma and Caspar dance around and around together.*)

Caspar at the Lost and Found Office

Characters
CASPAR MUFFIN POLICEMAN

CASPAR. (*Appearing in front of the curtain.*) Children, are you all there?

CHILDREN. Yes.

CASPAR. That's good! I'm glad you're there, because I'm *so* sad. Do you know why, children?

CHILDREN. No.

CASPAR. Well, I'll explain. It's because it's simply freezing here. Just like the North Pole! Do you know *how* cold it is at the North Pole?

CHILDREN. No.

CASPAR. It's so cold that if you have a drip at the end of your nose it turns into an icicle. Brrrr! Soon I'm going to have a very red Caspar nose. What a cold winter we're having this year—a real wooly-Caspar-cap-and-mittens winter! But the trouble is, children, that my lovely warm, wooly Caspar cap has disappeared. Yes . . . my lovely red, wooly, pointed Caspar cap. Gretel knit it for me, you know. Goodness knows where it is! I've been looking for it everywhere. You haven't seen it, have you, children?

CHILDREN. No.

CASPAR. Gretel hasn't seen it either, and neither has Grandma. But I've a pretty good idea what's happened to my winter, wooly Caspar cap. Some thief has stolen it! Pinched it! And hidden it somewhere. A burglar, probably, with a big black beard. Anyway, I'm going to see my good friend, the policeman, who lives around the corner, and I'm going to tell him all about this burglar with a big black beard. I hope the policeman is home. Anyway, Muffin will be there. Muffin is an even better friend of mine. He's a dog. He's the policeman's wire-haired terrier. When it's cold like it is now, Muffin never goes out. He doesn't like the cold. Children, are any of your friends dogs?

CHILDREN. Yes (and no).

CASPAR. Did I hear some of you say no? Perhaps you mean you think dogs don't count as friends because they can't talk? But Muffin *can* talk. You'll see! Muffin is cleverer than the policeman. He's a real detective. He'll be sure to discover who's taken my winter, wooly Caspar cap and hidden it! (*Exit.*)

The curtain goes up in the policeman's house. Muffin, looking very pleased with himself, is sitting in his basket (fastened to the stage ledge—the playboard).

MUFFIN. (*Sitting up as he hears a knock at the door.*) Come in!

CASPAR. (*Enters.*) Good morning, Muffin. All alone?

MUFFIN. Yes.

CASPAR. Is your master on duty?

MUFFIN. Yes.

CASPAR. Will he be home soon?

MUFFIN. Yes.

CASPAR. You're not very talkative today. I have something very important to discuss with you.

MUFFIN. Oh, yes?

CASPAR. My winter, wooly Caspar cap has disappeared. (*Muffin says nothing.*) Have you given up talking, Muffin? (*Muffin still says nothing.*) You didn't run to meet me today like you usually do. Why are you still sitting there in your basket?

MUFFIN. My front right paw has gone to sleep.

CASPAR. Really? May I listen to see if it's snoring? (*He approaches the basket.*)

MUFFIN. No, go away! You'll wake it up. I'll listen myself. (*Muffin tucks his head into the basket.*) Yes, it's snoring. (*Muffin snores.*) Can you hear it?

CASPAR. It snores just like you do!

MUFFIN. I don't snore. I've never heard myself snoring once.

CASPAR. But *I* have! This is how you snore. (*He snores.*)

MUFFIN. That's the way *you* snore!

CASPAR. I don't snore.

MUFFIN. But I've heard you snoring.

CASPAR. That must have been you.

MUFFIN. No, no! But it might have been my right front paw—the one that's asleep. Anyway, that's why I can't get out of my basket.

CASPAR. Well, anyway, you must help me to find out who's stolen my winter, wooly Caspar cap.

MUFFIN. Oh, we'll catch the thief soon.

POLICEMAN. (*Enters.*) What thief?

MUFFIN. The thief who's stolen Caspar's winter, wooly Caspar cap.

CASPAR. Yes. A big burglar with a big black beard.

POLICEMAN. And where did you lose your cap?

CASPAR. He took it from under my pillow. That's what must have happened.

POLICEMAN. When?

CASPAR. In the middle of the night! It must have been then.

POLICEMAN. Oh-ho! In the middle of the night, eh? You're sure it wasn't in the middle of the day?

CASPAR. No, in the middle of the day my cap's always on my head.

POLICEMAN. Was it on your head yesterday at three o'clock?

CASPAR. Of course it was!

POLICEMAN. Oh, that's a pity. Because it so happens that a lovely red, winter, wooly Caspar cap has been turned in at the Lost and Found Office. But that one had been dropped by someone at three in the afternoon yesterday on the frozen lake where everyone goes skating.

CASPAR. Well I never! I'd better go over to the Lost and Found Office then.

POLICEMAN. But that couldn't be *your* cap! What would your cap have been doing on the frozen lake in the middle of the afternoon?

CASPAR. Perhaps the burglar with the big black beard dropped it there?

POLICEMAN. Perhaps he picked it up on the frozen lake and took it to the Lost and Found Office.

CASPAR. But where *is* the Lost and Found Office?

POLICEMAN. In the corner, there . . . Muffin's basket is the Lost and Found Office.

CASPAR. (*Looking in the basket and tugging at a cap.*) Here it is! Here it is!

MUFFIN. (*Holding onto it.*) No, I want to keep it . . . it's so lovely and warm!

CASPAR. No, give it to me, it's *my* Caspar cap! (*They have a tug o'war with the cap.*)

POLICEMAN. That's enough, you rascals. You'll tear it to bits. You're a fine Lost and Found Office manager, Muffin! (*Muffin lets go of the cap.*) That's better. Lost property must always be returned to the owner.

MUFFIN. But there ought to be a reward for the finder.

CASPAR. Who *was* the finder?

MUFFIN. Me, of course!

POLICEMAN. What are you going to give Muffin as a reward, Caspar?

CASPAR. A cold sausage? Would that be all right, Muffin?

MUFFIN. Can I go with Caspar to buy the cold sausage?

POLICEMAN. Yes, but don't stay out too long, you big black-bearded burglar!

CASPAR. How glad I am to have my lovely red, warm, winter, wooly Caspar cap back. Now I won't have cold ears any more!

Caspar and Icicle Mike

Characters

CASPAR GRANDMA
MIKE SKATES

ICE (*voice only*)

CASPAR. (*Appearing in front of the curtain.*) Children, I want to ask you a riddle. It's quite a difficult riddle. What is it that falls in the winter when it's very cold? It falls on trees and houses and on children's heads. What is it—rain or snow?

CHILDREN. Snow.

CASPAR. And what can you do when there's a lot of snow?

CHILDREN. Make snowballs. Build snowmen.

CASPAR. And what else?

CHILDREN. Go sledding. Or skiing.

CASPAR. And when the ponds and lakes are frozen, what can you do then?

CHILDREN. Skate.

CASPAR. And when is it all right to skate? Is it all right the first day when the ice is only as thick as your little finger?

CHILDREN. No!

CASPAR. That's what I told my friend Mike. "Look out," I said. "With those brand-new skates you don't want to go swimming instead, do you!" Children, is it all right to skate when the ice is as thick as two fingers?

CHILDREN. No!

CASPAR. Three fingers?

CHILDREN. No!

CASPAR. Four fingers?

CHILDREN. Yes (and no).

CASPAR. Well, I think the ice should be as thick as five fingers, children, before you go skating. That's what I told my friend, Mike. But he wouldn't listen. Anyway, you'd better see for yourselves what happened to Mike and his new skates. Just a moment . . . (*Caspar disappears and the curtain goes up.*)

Mike and Grandma at home. A pair of shining new skates are standing in one corner. They are supported from below by stiff wires.

MIKE. Grandma, I've just thought of something.

GRANDMA. What have you just thought of, Mike?

MIKE. Er . . . I was just thinking . . . that you are the best Grandma in the world!

GRANDMA. I'd better watch out then, hadn't I!

MIKE. Why, Grandma?

GRANDMA. Because I happen to know why I'm suddenly the best Grandma in the world. (*She points to the skates.*) It's because of those skates.

MIKE. Yes. It's because you've given me the most beautiful skates in the world.

GRANDMA. But you must not go skating until I say you may.

MIKE. Dear Grandma, may I put on the radio? It's time for the weather forecast.

GRANDMA. Yes, do.

MIKE. (*Mike goes to the radio [painted at the side of the stage]. There is an announcement: "This is the weather forecast. Five degrees of frost are expected during the night." Mike turns it off.*) Hooray! More frost! Did you hear that, Skates? Soon we'll be able to go skating. (*He strokes them.*)

GRANDMA. Not before the day after tomorrow. Are you listening to me, Mike? And now you must do your homework while I do the shopping. (*Exit.*)

MIKE. I bet the ice would hold if I went skating today. Why should I wait until the day after tomorrow?

SKATES. (*Dancing up and down.*) Of course it would hold today!

MIKE. You can't wait either?

SKATES. (*Dancing.*) No, of course we can't!

MIKE. Perhaps we could just *try* it . . . the pond's not far.

SKATES. (*Dancing.*) Yes. Let's!

MIKE. Of course we'd stay close to the edge where the pond isn't deep. Would that make you happy?

SKATES. (*Dancing.*) Yes! Yes!

MIKE. But suppose we fell in?

SKATES. We wouldn't.

MIKE. All right, then. Let's go quickly, so that we're home again before Grandma gets back. (*Exit with skates.*)

>   Mike alone on the frozen pond. He is skating up and down. His feet are invisible.

MIKE. Oh, it's great fun! Ice like glass! Brand-new ice! As good as a brand-new car! No dents! No marks! It's like flying!

ICE. (*Creaking softly.*) Trust me! Trust me!

MIKE. I do trust you. But who said that?

ICE. (*Creaking again.*) Me. The ice. Just trust me!

MIKE. Don't I skate well! Ten yards from the edge already!

ICE. Just a little farther! Go on! Go on! (*It cracks noisily.*)

MIKE. Oh, I must get back.

ICE. Too late! Too late! (*A terrible rending sound.*)

MIKE. (*Up to his chest in the water and threshing around with his arms.*) Help! Help! (*He flounders back to the bank.*) Oh, I'm not drowned after all! But how cold I am! Brrr! I'd better get home quickly or I'll turn into an icicle. (*Exit.*)

    At Mike's house. Grandma comes in with her shopping basket.

GRANDMA. Mike, where are you? Skates, where are you?

MIKE. (*Staggering in.*) Here we are.

GRANDMA. Goodness! Come in quickly! Into the warm!

MIKE. I can't walk quickly. I've turned into an icicle.

GRANDMA. Ah! Now I understand. Take your clothes off at once and get into bed or you'll have a temperature tomorrow.

MIKE. It's no good! My clothes are frozen stiff. That stupid old ice. It's not my fault, it's the ice's fault.

GRANDMA. Oh, it is, is it! Then the ice deserves a good beating, doesn't it!

MIKE. I just want to get warm again.

GRANDMA. Lie down on the floor, Mike. (*She goes out with her basket and comes back with a rug-beater.*) Here we are! (*She beats him.*)

MIKE. Ow! Ow! Ow! Don't beat me!

GRANDMA. Oh, I wouldn't dream of beating *you*! I'm just beating that stupid old ice. You know you said it was all the ice's fault.

MIKE. Ow! Ow!

GRANDMA. (*Still beating him.*) I'll beat that stupid old ice to a jelly. Are you getting any warmer?

MIKE. Ow! Yes, my seat's quite hot now!

GRANDMA. That will upset the ice, won't it, if you get nice and warm. It'll melt! And you'd like that, wouldn't you?

MIKE. Oh, Grandma, please stop. It's *me* you're beating to a jelly!

GRANDMA. Of course I'm not. Just the ice—that stupid old ice. And now you'd better get right into bed so that you're well enough to go skating . . . the day after tomorrow!

MIKE. (*Standing up.*) May I go skating the day after tomorrow after all?

GRANDMA. I promised that you could . . . the day after tomorrow. As long as it stays freezing cold.

MIKE. I'll show that stupid old ice!

GRANDMA. That stupid old ice I've just beaten to a jelly?

MIKE. Thank you, dear Grandma. You're the best . . .

GRANDMA. Yes, you've said that before. And you're . . . you're . . .

MIKE. What am I, Grandma?

GRANDMA. You're the wettest icicle in the world! Aren't you?

MIKE. You bet!

CURTAIN.

CASPAR. (*Appearing in front of the curtain.*) I'm glad my friend Mike escaped from that stupid old ice, aren't you, children?

CHILDREN. Yes!

CASPAR. (*Shouts.*) You're glad too, aren't you, Mike?

MIKE. (*From behind the curtain.*) You bet!

CASPAR. How thick was the ice, Mike?

MIKE. Four fingers too thin!

CASPAR. Are you going swimming again tomorrow?

MIKE. No, I'm not going swimming again before next summer.

CASPAR. He's right, isn't he, children? Swimming's for summer. And skating's for days when the ice is thick enough. How many fingers have you got on each hand, children?

CHILDREN. Five (or four).

CASPAR. Five fingers . . . or four fingers and one thumb! That's right. Good-by for now, children.

Caspar and Bob the Robber

CHARACTERS

CASPAR **ROOSTER**
UNCLE **THREE HENS**
BOB THE ROBBER

CASPAR. (*Enters singing.*)
    In a cabin in a wood,
    Little man by a window stood.
    Saw a rabbit hopping by,
    Knocking at my door.
    "Help me! Help me! Help me!" he said,
    "Or that man will shoot me dead!"
    "Little rabbit, come inside.
    Safely you'll abide."
Did you like that song, children?

CHILDREN. Yes.

CASPAR. Shall I sing you an even nicer song?

CHILDREN. Yes.

CASPAR. But I'd like my uncle, the forest ranger, to sing it with me. I'm spending my vacation with him. Come and sing the Rabbit Song with me, Uncle.

UNCLE. The Rabbit Song? Oh yes . . . but let's act it too.

CASPAR. Act it? Why, yes, of course! That'll be much more fun. It will be the best song in the world. (*Caspar and Uncle sing the song together and do the appropriate actions. They draw a cabin in the air, catch sight of the rabbit, run up, knock on the door, and so on, all in time to the music. They sing together or take turns. Perhaps Caspar can persuade the children to join in.*)

CASPAR. You sang very well, Uncle.

UNCLE. I did my best. But I'm not in the mood for singing today. I've lost another hen. That's the sixth out of my nine hens.

CASPAR. Oh, dear! So you've only got one, two, three hens and a fine rooster, instead of three times three hens and a fine rooster!

UNCLE. Yes. But I know who the thief is.

CASPAR. So do I. (*Sings.*)
    Fox, I know you've stolen a hen.
    Kindly give her back again.

UNCLE. No! No!

CASPAR. You don't want the fox to give the hens back?

UNCLE. It wasn't the fox.

CASPAR. Who was it then?

UNCLE. Can you tell one animal track from another?

CASPAR. Of course I can. Fox tracks and badger tracks, cat tracks and rat tracks and squirrel tracks—I know them all.

UNCLE. And whose tracks are these? (*Points step by step to a set of tracks.*)

CASPAR. (*Looking step by step at the tracks.*) Help! Help!

UNCLE. What's got into you? Did someone stick a pin in you?

CASPAR. Worse than that! There's only one person with feet as big as this . . . Bob the Robber!

UNCLE. You *are* good at tracking! But how are we going to catch this robber?

CASPAR. Simple! I'll stay awake tonight and surprise him.

UNCLE. You? Stay awake? You snore like a dragon as soon as your head touches the pillow.

CASPAR. Then your dog Trigger could catch him.

UNCLE. Trigger snores all night like a mini-dragon.

CASPAR. What about *you* then, Uncle?

UNCLE. Me? I snore like a giant dragon.

CASPAR. I know someone who doesn't snore at all at night—that rooster.

UNCLE. But it's all his fault in the first place! He was in the henhouse when the robber came. Did he crow?

CASPAR. He did not!

UNCLE. Well, he'll have to pay for it. He'll have to be punished. Go and get him.

CASPAR. Right, Uncle. (*Exit and returns with the rooster.*) Here he is!

ROOSTER. Cock-a-doodle-doo! Let me go! Let me go!

UNCLE. Hold him tight! He's working with the robber.

ROOSTER. Cock-a-doodle-doo! Not guilty! Not guilty!

CASPAR. Why didn't you crow when the robber stole into the henhouse?

ROOSTER. I was afraid. Cock-a-doodle-doo! He stole in and wrung one of the hens' necks and before you could say cock-a-doodle-doo he'd run away.

UNCLE. Why didn't he take you, too?

ROOSTER. Ha ha! I was sitting at the back on the perch.

CASPAR. And why weren't you out in front which is where you should have been?

ROOSTER. I was afraid. Cock-a-doodle-doo! He might have wrung *my* neck.

UNCLE. I see! Well, I'm going to wring your neck now.

ROOSTER. Oh, no! Please don't. I'll catch the robber.

CASPAR. How? With your cock-a-doodle-doo?

ROOSTER. Without it first. And then with it.

UNCLE. Well, you'd better watch out, Cock-a-doodle-doo! Because if you don't catch the robber there'll be roast chicken next Sunday.

ROOSTER. No, there won't be, there won't be. Cock-a-doodle-doo! I'll catch him all right.

CASPAR. I wonder if there *will* be roast chicken next Sunday.

On the left a henhouse with a big bolt on the door. Inside three hens and, on the far left, the rooster. It is almost dark.

FIRST HEN. The robber's coming for me today. Cluck, cluck!

SECOND HEN. And tomorrow he's coming for *me*. Cluck, cluck!

THIRD HEN. And the day after for *me*. Cluck, cluck!

ROOSTER. He's not going to get any of you. Cock-a-doodle-doo!

FIRST HEN. It's all very well for you to talk. You're hiding at the back.

ROOSTER. (*Flapping to the front.*) Cock-a-doodle-doo! I'm not hiding now.

FIRST HEN. Goodness, what a surprise! Cluck, cluck!

SECOND HEN. Goodness! Cluck, cluck!

THIRD HEN. Will the robber get you instead? Cluck, cluck!

ROOSTER. No. *I* will get *him*. What do you make of that?

FIRST HEN. Nothing at all. Cluck, cluck!

SECOND HEN. Nothing. Cluck, cluck!

THIRD HEN. *How* will you get him?

ROOSTER. I will crow at him. Cock-a-doodle-doo! But *you* have to keep quiet. He's coming now. (*The hens retreat to the back of the henhouse, the rooster remaining in front. Bob the Robber creeps up, slides the big bolt back carefully, opens the door and climbs in.*) Good evening, Bob the Robber. (*The robber draws his hand back and is about to run away.*) Don't go, Bob. There's nobody here.

ROBBER. Who are you, then?

ROOSTER. Your friend, the rooster.

ROBBER. *Are* you my friend?

ROOSTER. Of course! After all, you haven't wrung *my* neck, have you?

ROBBER. Er . . . no. But where are the hens?

ROOSTER. On the perch at the back. I'll make room for you to come in and get them.

ROBBER. That's very kind of you.

ROOSTER. Well, I'm your friend, aren't I? (*Hops out of henhouse.*)

ROBBER. And I'll never wring *your* neck.

ROOSTER. That's very kind of you.

ROBBER. Well, I'm your friend. (*He creeps into the henhouse.*)

ROOSTER. (*Slamming the henhouse door behind him.*) Now I've bolted the door so that no one can steal *you*! Cock-a-doodle-doo! Cock-a-doodle-doo!

ROBBER. Shut up! Open the door! Open the door! (*He bangs his head against the door.*)

ROOSTER. I've got him! I've caught the robber.

UNCLE. (*Comes in with Caspar.*) Where is he?

ROOSTER. Inside.

CASPAR. Oh, dear! No roast chicken after all.

ROOSTER. That's *not* very kind of you.

CASPAR. Oh, it was just a joke! From today I'm *really* your friend because you've caught the robber.

ROOSTER. I'm glad.

UNCLE. How are you getting along in the henhouse, Bob the Robber?

ROBBER. (*Choking with rage, he makes a sound like "cluck, cluck."*)

CASPAR. Why are you cackling like a hen?

UNCLE. What are you trying to say, Bob?

ROBBER. Nothing you'll want to hear.

UNCLE. What shall we do with the robber now?

HENS. Let him out! Cluck, cluck!

ROOSTER. No, keep him in! Cock-a-doodle-doo!

HENS. Out! Cluck, cluck!

ROOSTER. In! Cock-a-doodle-doo!

UNCLE. What do you think, Caspar?

CASPAR. Out! Cluck, cluck!

ROOSTER. Let him out? But he's a robber.

CASPAR. Let him out so he can be locked up. Cock-a-doodle-doo!

ROOSTER. Oh yes! That's a good idea. I'll go to get the policeman.

CASPAR. And we'll sing our song to the robber. All right, Uncle? Just so that he doesn't get bored.

UNCLE. Do you know the Rabbit Song, Bob?

ROBBER. No, I don't . . . and I don't want to, either!

CASPAR. Oh, but you'll like it. Do please listen! (*Caspar and Uncle sing and act the Rabbit Song, this time with slightly different words.*)
> In a cabin in a wood,
> Robber Bob at the window stood.
> Saw a policeman coming by,
> Knocking at my door.

ROBBER. (*Adding the last line.*) Help me, help me, help me!

CASPAR. Why, he *does* know the Rabbit Song. He's joining in. Perhaps we ought to let him go.

UNCLE. Certainly not! But what do you think, children? Should you let a robber go?

CHILDREN. No.

CASPAR. Are you afraid of the robber?

CHILDREN. No.

CASPAR. Would you be afraid if he was coming to get you?

CHILDREN. We'd run away.

CASPAR. You don't need to run away, children. The robber's going to have a long vacation. And he's probably going to stay indoors for quite a while. But we'll meet again very soon, won't we, children?

Caspar and the Green Rabbits

Characters

CASPAR RABBIT
UNCLE FOX
OWL KING OF THE WOOD
TWO GREEN RABBITS

Outside the forest ranger's house.

CASPAR. What fun it is staying with my uncle, the forest ranger! Do *you* enjoy vacations too, children?

CHILDREN. Yes!

CASPAR. But there are two snags about vacations, aren't there? One before and one after. Which of you knows what those two snags are? Nobody? Well, I'll tell you. The snag before is that the vacation starts too late. Right?

CHILDREN. Yes.

CASPAR. And the snag after is that it ends . . .

CHILDREN. Too soon!

CASPAR. Right. But apart from that, vacations are great! Especially if you can stay with an uncle who's a forest ranger. I always go everywhere with my uncle. Except today when he's out chasing rabbits. I don't like that at all—all those men and dogs after a few poor rabbits. (*Uncle enters.*) Hello, Uncle. How did it go?

UNCLE. (*Crossly.*) I want to read my paper.

CASPAR. How many rabbits did you catch?

UNCLE. (*Crosser than ever.*) None at all!

CASPAR. (*Impetuously.*) Oh, good! Er . . . I mean, why was that?

UNCLE. Not one in sight.

CASPAR. How peculiar!

UNCLE. I don't know what's happened to them.

CASPAR. But perhaps *I* do! Uncle . . . why are snowshoe rabbits white in winter?

UNCLE. To match the snow.

CASPAR. And you can't see them because they're as white as the snow.

UNCLE. Right.

CASPAR. Well, then. You couldn't see any rabbits today because they're grass rabbits, as green as the grass. That's it—the rabbits around here are green rabbits.

UNCLE. No, they're not.

CASPAR. But if there are white rabbits, why shouldn't there be green ones?

UNCLE. (*Very annoyed.*) That's nonsense!

CASPAR. You're not in a very good mood today, Uncle.

UNCLE. Not a rabbit in sight. And now I can't find my *Sporting Times*.

CASPAR. Does it usually say in the *Sporting Times* when there's to be a rabbit hunt?

UNCLE. Yes.

CASPAR. When was the last time you saw your paper?

UNCLE. Last night. It's been disappearing every day before I've hardly glanced at it. (*Stamps off angrily.*)

CASPAR. That's very peculiar, isn't it! I'll keep a look-out tonight in the wood. Perhaps I'll discover who's taking Uncle's paper.

That night. In the wood.

CASPAR. (*Enters, whistling.*) Is anyone there? A thief, for instance?

OWL. (*Invisible.*) There aren't any thieves in this wood.

CASPAR. Who said that?

OWL. (*Enters.*) Me! Owl! Good evening, Caspar. Nice to see you.

CASPAR. Good evening, Owl.

OWL. Why were you whistling like that at night in the wood?

CASPAR. Oh . . . just because . . .

OWL. I thought it might be because you were afraid.

CASPAR. Well, anyone can be wrong, can't he?

OWL. There's nothing for Caspar to be afraid of, is there, Rabbit?

RABBIT. (*Enters.*) Of course not! We're all Caspar's friends here. Good evening, Caspar. Nice to see you.

CASPAR. Good evening, Rabbit. I'm so glad none of you were caught yesterday.

OWL. And no one knows why not.

RABBIT. May we let Caspar into the secret?

OWL. Of course. He's our friend.

RABBIT. Then listen, Caspar . . .

OWL. Just a minute. You can see for yourself, Caspar.

FOX. (*Entering with a newspaper between his front paws.*) Good evening, Caspar. Nice to see you.

CASPAR. Good evening, Fox. But isn't that the *Sporting Times*?

FOX. Yes. We get it free from your uncle, the forest ranger.

CASPAR. Can you read?

FOX. I can't myself. I'm just the paper boy. But Owl can read.

RABBIT. Please tell us what it says today, Owl.

OWL. (*Looking at the newspaper which is held up by Fox and Rabbit.*) Oh dear! They're at it again.

RABBIT. Is there something about rabbits?

OWL. No—it's about foxes this time.

FOX. Please read us the news, Owl—the news about foxes.

OWL. (*Reading.*) "The countryside is overrun with foxes and these animals are getting bolder and bolder. Something must be done."

FOX. (*Dropping the newspaper.*) Oh dear! They're going to do away with us.

CASPAR. Someone else was saying that to me yesterday.

FOX. Who?

CASPAR. Uncle's geese and hens. They were talking about you!

FOX. Well, I can't be expected to starve to death.

CASPAR. Couldn't you manage with mice?

FOX. The cats need all the mice.

CASPAR. Fox dear, is it true that there are green foxes?

FOX. (*Indignantly.*) Certainly not!

CASPAR. You sound like my uncle. But I *know* there are green rabbits. Rabbits you can't see in the grass.

RABBIT. What makes you think that?

CASPAR. Yesterday when they were out hunting, they didn't see a single rabbit, so I told my uncle it must be because the rabbits were all green and they couldn't see them in the grass.

RABBIT, FOX and OWL. (*Laughing.*) Ha ha ha! Green rabbits! That's a good one.

RABBIT. (*Recovering himself.*) I must tell the other rabbits that! (*Exit.*)

FOX. I must tell the other foxes that. (*Gives Caspar the paper.*) Here, Caspar . . . please give this back to your uncle. I'm finished with it now. (*Exit.*)

OWL. And I must tell the other owls that . . . the whole wood, in fact! (*Exit.*)

CASPAR. So much for my green rabbits! They've all run away and left me.

KING OF THE WOOD. (*Enters.*) The whole wood is laughing about your green rabbits.

CASPAR. Who are you, then?

KING OF THE WOOD. I'm King of this wood. I'll grant you one wish because you've made the whole wood laugh.

CASPAR. Oh, that's wonderful. Then I wish for . . . a green rabbit.

KING OF THE WOOD. I suppose you couldn't possibly wish for something else? Green rabbits are rather difficult.

CASPAR. No. Sorry.

TWO GREEN RABBITS. (*Hopping onto the stage.*) Here we are! (*The rabbits are wearing green leaves.*)

KING OF THE WOOD. Goodness gracious! How long have you been in my wood?

RABBITS. Ever since Caspar invented us. (*They speak alternate lines.*)
    At first we rabbits laughed and laughed
    And thought the whole idea quite daft.
    But now, dear Caspar, just for you,
    We're here to make your wish come true.

CASPAR. Thank you *very* much, dear Rabbits. You've made me very happy. But, I tell you what . . . could you come again tomorrow morning to see my uncle?

RABBITS. Wouldn't that be rather dangerous?

CASPAR. Not if I'm there too.

RABBITS. Should we go to see Caspar's uncle, Your Majesty?

KING OF THE WOOD. So long as Caspar's there too.

CASPAR. See you tomorrow morning then. Good-by for now, Rabbits.

RABBITS. Good-by for now, Caspar.

CASPAR. Good-by, Your Majesty.

KING OF THE WOOD. Come to see us again soon, Caspar.

   Outside the forest ranger's house.

CASPAR. Honestly, Uncle, there *are* green rabbits.

UNCLE. There aren't!

CASPAR. But I've seen them with my own eyes.

UNCLE. When was that?

CASPAR. Last night.

UNCLE. You must have dreamed it.

CASPAR. The owl was reading your *Sporting Times*.

UNCLE. That settles it! Of course you were dreaming. How could the owl have gotten hold of my paper?

CASPAR. The fox took it for him.

UNCLE. But there it is in your hand! You're holding it yourself.

CASPAR. Yes. I brought it back with me from the wood. The fox asked me to give it to you since he was finished with it.

UNCLE. What nonsense! I must have dropped it in the wood.

CASPAR. Uncle, can you tell one animal's track from another's?

UNCLE. Of course I can!

CASPAR. Well, this one on the right—what's that? (*Shows newspaper.*)

UNCLE. A rabbit.

CASPAR. That was the rabbit who came to take your paper the day before yesterday. And this one on the left?

UNCLE. A fox.

CASPAR. That was the fox who came to take your paper yesterday.

UNCLE. At this rate we'll be seeing a couple of green rabbits any moment now!

TWO GREEN RABBITS. (*Hopping onto the stage.*) Good morning all.

UNCLE. Good heavens! I must tell the *Sporting Times* about this . . . I'd better call the editor. This is a front-page story!

RABBITS AND CASPAR. (*They speak alternate lines, Rabbits first.*)
    Today's a day we'll not regret.
    A day my uncle won't forget!
    Back to the woods now. Cheerio!
    Another dance before you go.

RABBITS. All right, Caspar. We'll do anything for you.

CASPAR. (*Sings a cheerful song while the rabbits dance around together.*)

Caspar in the Desert

Characters

CASPAR COCO THE AFRICAN
UNCLE NICK SIMBO THE LION

CASPAR. (*Enters singing.*)
  Tra la la! Tra la la!
  Here we are! Here we are!
Children, I'm very happy today. I'm on vacation. So I'm jumping for joy. (*Does this.*) But that's nothing. Last week I jumped fifteen thousand feet in the air. Do you believe that, children?

CHILDREN. No!

CASPAR. I did, you know.

CHILDREN. You couldn't have.

CASPAR. Yes, I did. And when I came back to earth I was at the North Pole. Brrr! It was *so* cold. It makes me shiver just to think of it. All those polar bears and icebergs and igloos! I nearly froze to death. (*Shivers and hugs himself miserably.*) Shall I tell you how I really got to the North Pole?

CHILDREN. Yes.

CASPAR. I went with my Uncle Nick. He's an airline pilot. And when he has his day off, he takes me by plane wherever I want to go. Do you believe me now?

CHILDREN. Yes.

CASPAR. Uncle Nick didn't want to go to the North Pole because it's so cold there. But I was very obstinate. I wanted to go to the North Pole and nowhere else would do. But today we can go somewhere else. Shall I tell you where I want to go today?

CHILDREN. Yes.

CASPAR. I want to go somewhere really warm! Somewhere blazing hot! Where there are dates and bananas and coconuts. Which hot place should we go to, children, to find dates and bananas and coconuts?

CHILDREN. Africa.

CASPAR. Right. We're going to the Sahara Desert in Africa. With Uncle Nick. (*The roar of an airplane.*) He's coming now.

UNCLE NICK. (*Landing in his plane.*) Jump in, Caspar. I've had an idea. Let's go to Turkey and eat Turkish candy.

CASPAR. No. It gives me a toothache.

UNCLE NICK. Where shall we go then?

CASPAR. Let's go where there are dates and bananas and coconuts.

UNCLE NICK. Dates don't give you a toothache?

CASPAR. No! Never!

UNCLE NICK. All right then. We'll fly to a date island, and then to a banana island and then to a coconut island.

CASPAR. I'm not keen on islands. There's so much water around them. I'd like to go to the desert where it's blazing hot.

UNCLE NICK. The desert's even nastier than the North Pole. It's full of sand.

CASPAR. That's all right.

UNCLE NICK. And sand flies. They're even worse!

CASPAR. I don't mind.

UNCLE NICK. We might meet a stray lion.

CASPAR. I don't mind.

UNCLE NICK. Well, all right. Jump in! But don't blame me if you get bitten by a sand fly . . . or a lion!

CASPAR. (*Jumping into the plane.*) I won't mind.

UNCLE NICK. Well, we'll see. (*The plane takes off.*)

In the desert. The plane lands noisily. (It must be fastened to the back of the playboard.) Uncle Nick stays in it but Caspar climbs out.

UNCLE NICK. Here we are. In the desert! Is it warm enough for you?

CASPAR. Yes! It's great! (*He flops down.*) It's quite different from the North Pole, isn't it? No icebergs.

UNCLE NICK. Only sand.

CASPAR. No Polar bears.

UNCLE NICK. And no dates or bananas or coconuts either, as far as I can see!

CASPAR. That doesn't matter. I'm not at all hungry. (*He begins to scratch.*)

UNCLE NICK. But there seem to be a few guaranteed genuine desert sand flies around!

CASPAR. (*Scratches more vigorously.*) They bite!

UNCLE NICK. What a pity there isn't a monkey about. He'd get rid of them for you.

CASPAR. Couldn't *you* get rid of them for me, Uncle?

UNCLE NICK. You don't seem to like the desert so much after all.

CASPAR. No. I don't like it a bit. It's all the fault of these guaranteed nasty desert sand flies.

UNCLE NICK. Well, let's fly off to the date island.

CASPAR. I must have a good scratch first. They're biting me everywhere. (*He scratches. A lion roars.*) What was that?

UNCLE NICK. A guaranteed genuine lion's roar! Quick—jump back in the plane!

CASPAR. (*Runs toward the plane, followed by the lion. The engine starts, coughs, and stops again. The lion retreats momentarily but then advances toward the plane again.*) Help! Help! That lion wants to bite me!

COCO. (*Enters.*) Don't worry! The lion won't bite you. My name is Coco, by the way. (*He bows.*)

CASPAR. And I'm Caspar. (*He bows.*)

UNCLE NICK. And I'm Uncle Nick. (*He bows too.*)

COCO. My lion's name is Simbo. (*The lion bows too.*) He's my house-lion.

UNCLE NICK. I've never heard of a house-lion.

COCO. He looks after things when I'm out. He's very obliging. Is there anything you'd like him to do for you?

CASPAR. (*Doubtfully.*) Could he find me a banana?

COCO. In the twinkling of an eye. Simbo! Banana! (*Simbo rushes off and returns with a banana in his jaws. He offers it to Caspar.*) Please accept it with Simbo's best wishes.

CASPAR. Do you think it's safe for me to take it, Uncle? I'm so hungry.

UNCLE NICK. Yes, I'm sure it's safe if Coco says so.

CASPAR. (*Moves with some hesitation toward Simbo and takes the banana.*) Thank you very much, dear Simbo.

COCO. You see what a nice lion he is!

CASPAR. Yes. But he didn't seem quite so nice at first. He rushed up and frightened us.

COCO. He was upset because you wanted to fly away. He was hoping you'd stay and play with him.

CASPAR. Let's play tag, then, Simbo. (*Caspar runs away, and Simbo, growling playfully, follows and catches him.*) Help! Help! He's caught me.

COCO. He won't hurt you, Caspar. *You* chase *him* now.

CASPAR. (*Chases the lion and catches him.*) I like it here, after all, Uncle Nick. Let's stay!

COCO. Oh yes! Do stay! Then Simbo will always have someone to play with.

CASPAR. (*Starting to scratch.*) No . . . I think perhaps I'd rather not.

COCO. Oh, I see! Because of the . . .

CASPAR. . . . guaranteed nasty desert sand flies! No, I can't bear it, even though it *is* so lovely and warm here.

COCO. But look at poor Simbo. He's *so* disappointed.

CASPAR. I'm sorry. But we simply must leave.

UNCLE NICK. I've had an idea . . . Simbo could come with us! (*Simbo jumps happily into the plane.*) And Coco too, of course!

COCO. I'm jumping for joy! (*He jumps into the plane too.*)

CASPAR. Is there still room for me?

UNCLE NICK. Plenty of room. Jump in! (*Caspar jumps in.*)

COCO. Give the starting signal, Simbo! (*Simbo roars and the engine starts.*)

CASPAR. Just a moment! (*Uncle Nick switches off the engine.*) I've had an idea.

UNCLE NICK. What idea?

CASPAR. We could go home and get . . .

UNCLE NICK. What could we get?

CASPAR. A can of guaranteed genuine fly-repellent!

COCO. What a good idea! And then we can come back here. Give the starting signal again, Simbo. (*Simbo roars.*)

UNCLE NICK. But first we must go home! (*The plane takes off.*)

Caspar and the Magic Feather

Characters

CASPAR FEATHER
CLOCK GRANDMA

A clockface with two movable hands is painted at the right of the stage.

CASPAR. (*Enters from the left with a cushion. He puts it down, lays his head on it, and stretches out.*) It's awful when you haven't had enough sleep and your Grandma gets you out of bed at six in the morning, isn't it!

CLOCK. Actually, it's five minutes to twelve.

CASPAR. (*Rubbing his eyes.*) Who are you? A clock?

CLOCK. Right.

CASPAR. And you can talk!

CLOCK. Right.

CASPAR. Did you say it was almost twelve o'clock? Are you sure you're right?

CLOCK. Of course I'm right!

CASPAR. It can't be twelve already.

CLOCK. You don't think it's as late as that.

CASPAR. No. I think it's twice as late.

CLOCK. Do you expect me to strike thirteen or something?

CASPAR. Thirteen plus eleven. How much does that make—thirteen plus eleven?

CLOCK. I can't work it out.

CASPAR. Children, you must help him. How much is thirteen plus eleven?

CHILDREN. Twenty-four.

CASPAR. Got it, Clock?

CLOCK. You mean you think it's twenty-four hours, or twelve midnight?

CASPAR. Of course. And I can go back to bed for another six hours. (*Starts to walk off.*)

CLOCK. Caspar! Is it light or dark at twelve midnight?

CASPAR. Dark, of course! What a silly question!

CLOCK. And is it light or dark now?

CASPAR. Light, of course! What a silly question!

CLOCK. And so . . . oh, excuse me for a moment . . . (*He strikes twelve.*)

CASPAR. (*Counting out loud.*) One, two, three, four, five, six, seven, eight, nine, ten, eleven, twelve . . . twelve o'clock precisely!

CLOCK. Noon. You can tell that from my hands.

CASPAR. Do your hands always tell the right time?

CLOCK. Of course they do!

CASPAR. That's good.

CLOCK. What's so good about it?

CASPAR. Just you wait! (*He turns the hands back until they point to six o'clock.*) There! Now it's just six o'clock in the morning and I'm going to go and tell Grandma it's much too early to get up. (*Starts to walk off.*)

CLOCK. Caspar! Wait a minute! (*The hands turn around by themselves until they are pointing again to twelve o'clock.*) You see? You can't put the clock back!

CASPAR. Oh, what a pity. So I haven't time today to go on my ship to the pineapple island or to the land of the Eskimos where they don't have pineapples, but they do have popsicles.

CLOCK. You don't have a ship.

CASPAR. Yes, I have. Let me whisper . . . where is your ear, please?

CLOCK. You may speak into my keyhole . . . where they wind me up.

CASPAR. (*Whispers to the clock.*)

CLOCK. You think your bed is a ship! What nonsense! It stays in one place like a table.

CASPAR. Not when I shut my eyes! I can go anywhere then. My ship makes the most fabulous voyages. That's why I hate getting up. This morning I was just off to the pineapple island and to the land of the Eskimos when Grandma came in and put a stop to it.

CLOCK. It was high time you got up.

CASPAR. But today is the first day of my vacation.

CLOCK. There are many useful things you can do during a vacation.

CASPAR. Oh, dear!

CLOCK. You could spring-clean your bedroom, for example.

CASPAR. Oh, dear!

CLOCK. Or go out and buy the potatoes for your Grandma.

CASPAR. I don't think you're a very nice clock. I will take you into another room. (*Carries the clock away and returns without it.*) Pineapples are very much nicer than clocks, aren't they, children?

CHILDREN. Yes.

CASPAR. And so are popsicles, aren't they?

CHILDREN. Yes.

CASPAR. Do you know how to get a pineapple for nothing?

CHILDREN. No.

CASPAR. Or how to get a free popsicle?

CHILDREN. No.

CASPAR. What a shame! (*He sits down on the left.*) Anyway, even if I'm not allowed to stay in bed, I can still have a little more sleep . . . just a little . . . more . . . (*His head sinks on his chest. Then a white feather [supported on a stiff wire] hops up. [Later note paper and a pineapple can be brought on in the same way.] The feather tickles Caspar's nose.*) Atishoo! Who's tickling my nose?

FEATHER. Me!

CASPAR. Who's me?

FEATHER. I am.

CASPAR. Which I are you?

FEATHER. I'm me. (*The feather dances under Caspar's nose.*) I'm a magic feather. The person who sees me has to wish.

CASPAR. How nice! And how beautifully you dance!

FEATHER.
    I can hop and dance and fly
    Or in a corner quiet lie,
    Tickle a nose, or, even better,
    I can write a splendid letter.

Would you like me to write a letter for you? If not, I won't bother.

CASPAR. Well, the difficulty is that I don't have any note paper.

FEATHER. Oh, there's no difficulty there. This way, wind, this way— note paper, please. (*A pad of note paper swings across the stage.*)

Good. Now please hold the pad still so that I can write properly. Who are we writing to?

CASPAR. Could we write to the pineapple island and ask them to send me a pineapple?

FEATHER. All you have to do is dictate.

CASPAR. Dear Pineapple Island . . . (*The feather dances across the pad.*) Please send me a nice big pineapple. Many thanks and love from Caspar.

FEATHER. Is that all? (*Caspar nods happily.*) I'll send it by lightning mail—it'll get there quicker than a cable.

CASPAR. And what about the pineapple?

FEATHER. That'll come by lightning mail too. But only if you shut your eyes.

CASPAR. They're shut already. (*He lays his head on the playboard.*)

FEATHER. And you mustn't open them again until I tell you. Not an instant before.

CASPAR. But how will I see the pineapple?

FEATHER. You'll see it all right. It's coming now. (A *pineapple flies in.*)

CASPAR. Oh, a lovely pineapple! Is it mine?

FEATHER. Yes, it's all yours.

CASPAR. Then I'm going to cut myself a slice right away!

FEATHER. Not yet, Caspar! Keep your eyes shut!

CASPAR. I can't wait any longer. (*He jumps up and tries to catch the pineapple but it flies away from him.*) Ohhh!

FEATHER. Why did you open your eyes?

CASPAR. My beautiful pineapple!

FEATHER. Oh, well . . . we can write another letter. Shall we write this time to the land of the Eskimos and ask for a popsicle?

CASPAR. Oh, yes, please.

FEATHER. This way, wind, this way—note paper, please. (*The pad of note paper sails toward them and Caspar catches it.*) Now hold it still, please, and dictate your letter.

CASPAR. Dear Land of the Eskimos . . . (*The feather writes.*) Please send

me a popsicle immediately. Many thanks and much love from Caspar.

FEATHER. Off you go to the land of the Eskimos! (*The letter sails off.*)

CASPAR. This time I'll keep my eyes tight shut.

FEATHER. Then you'll be able to have as many licks as you like.

CASPAR. Good!

FEATHER. If you think it tastes good, will you let your Grandma have a lick too?

CASPAR. Well . . . she got me out of bed very early this morning.

FEATHER. But apart from that she's very good to you, isn't she? So may she have a lick?

CASPAR. Just one.

FEATHER. Three!

CASPAR. Two!

FEATHER. All right then—two. Are your eyes shut so that you can't see anything?

CASPAR. (*His head sunk on his chest.*) Nothing at all.

FEATHER. Oh, what's this? A *huge* popsicle. Look, Caspar! You can open your eyes now.

CASPAR. I'd rather not, or it may disappear.

FEATHER. Please yourself, but I'm off . . . (*Exit.*)

CASPAR. (*His head still bowed.*) Oh, what a lovely popsicle! A giant popsicle! Straight from the land of the Eskimos!

GRANDMA. (*Comes in with a popsicle and shakes her head. She speaks to the children.*) Caspar doesn't know that I've brought him a popsicle because it's the first day of his vacation! (*She steals up to Caspar and holds the popsicle under his nose.*)

CASPAR. I mustn't open my eyes. If I do the popsicle will disappear just like the pineapple did!

GRANDMA. This popsicle won't disappear. I'm holding it tight.

CASPAR. Are you sure, Grandma?

GRANDMA. Quite sure!

CASPAR. Then I'll open my eyes. Oh, isn't that a lovely popsicle, Grandma!

GRANDMA. Where do you think it came from, Caspar?

CASPAR. The magic feather sent a lightning letter to the land of the Eskimos, and the Eskimos sent me the popsicle.

GRANDMA. Fancy that! And to think that I was going to give you a popsicle because it's the first day of your vacation.

CASPAR. But now *I* can give *you* a popsicle—or, rather, we can each have a lot of licks. Would you like a lick too, children?

CHILDREN. Yes.

CASPAR. But I don't think there's enough for all of us. Sorry, children!

CURTAIN

CASPAR. (*Appearing in front of the curtain.*) I'll give you all a popsicle next time we meet . . . perhaps! (*He disappears but comes out once more.*) Maybe I will! Do you know when the next time will be?

CHILDREN. No.

CASPAR. The day after the day after the day after tomorrow. Is that too late?

CHILDREN. Yes.

CASPAR. Would you rather it was the day before the day before the day before yesterday?

CHILDREN. No.

CASPAR. Goodness, you're hard to please! Good-by for now, children!

Caspar and the Giant Fog

Characters

CASPAR
GRETEL (*in three sizes*)
SIGNPOST
GRANDMA
GIANT FOG

At Caspar's house. A table stands in one corner with a telephone on it.

CASPAR. I'm going to see my friend Fred now.

GRETEL. But, Caspar . . . you're not going out in this thick fog?

CASPAR. I don't care about the fog!

GRETEL. You'd have to cross the stream and you might fall in.

CASPAR. I don't care!

GRETEL. It'll be dark soon.

CASPAR. I don't care!

GRETEL. And I was looking forward to our playing a game together.

CASPAR. What game?

GRETEL. Hide-and-seek?

CASPAR. That's boring.

GRETEL. Or hopscotch?

CASPAR. Even more boring.

GRETEL. Or we could have a tug o'war with a jelly apple for the one who wins?

CASPAR. I always win.

GRETEL. Well, what are you going to play with your friend Fred?

CASPAR. A game.

GRETEL. What game?

CASPAR. Oh, I don't know . . . hide-and-seek perhaps.

GRETEL. I thought you said that was boring.

CASPAR. Or tug-a-jelly-apple with a war for the winner.

GRETEL. That's silly.

CASPAR. I'm going to take the "Hello-who's-there?" game with me. (*He picks up the telephone.*) I'll be back by seven.

GRETEL. And I know why too—because there are going to be pancakes for supper.

CASPAR. Twenty-two of them! Grandma told me. One for each of you, and twenty for me!

GRETEL. If you'd stay and play with me instead, you could have my pancake as well.

CASPAR. Thanks . . . but twenty will be enough. (*Exit.*)

GRETEL. (*Crying.*) I don't like you any more.

GRANDMA. (*Enters.*) Why are you crying, Gretel?

GRETEL. He's gone to play with his friend Fred again.

GRANDMA. He'll be back in time for the pancakes.

GRETEL. Is he really going to have twenty?

GRANDMA. Is *that* what he thinks? There are six pancakes, two each for the three of us, and if he's not back on the stroke of seven there'll be three each for the two of us—just you and me.

GRETEL. But suppose he was only about ten minutes late?

GRANDMA. It would make no difference if it was only *five* minutes.

GRETEL. He might lose his way in the fog.

GRANDMA. Nobody forced him to go out.

GRETEL. He might get stuck in the fog.

GRANDMA. Then we'd go and rescue him tomorrow morning.

GRETEL. Suppose he fell into the stream in the fog?

GRANDMA. Then he wouldn't need a bath tomorrow.

GRETEL. Suppose the Giant Fog caught him!

GRANDMA. Too bad!

GRETEL. I think I'd better go to meet him.

GRANDMA. No, we don't want the Giant catching you.

GRETEL. I'll take a lantern with me so that nothing can happen to Caspar.

In the fog by the stream.

GIANT FOG. (*A white ghost with flowing veils.*) This is where *I* live . . . by the stream. I am the Giant Fog. This time I'll catch Caspar. I'm going to blow more fog in the direction of his friend Fred's house . . . Pufffff! And toward Caspar's house . . . Pufffff! Fog all the way . . . Pufffff! And the thickest fog here by the stream . . . Pufffff! This time he'll fall in. This time I'll lead him around and around in circles! This time I'll have him gibbering with fright! It's nearly seven o'clock . . . Pufffff! And almost dark already . . . Pufffff! Thick, white fog . . . Pufffff! What lovely gray darkness! And Caspar doesn't have a lantern tonight . . . Ha ha ha!

Beside a signpost. Wisps of fog are hanging around it.

CASPAR. Oh, dear! I'm lost in the fog. I won't be back in time for the pancakes. Hello! Hello! Does anyone know which is the way to Caspar's house? Information, please! (*He dials on the tele-*

phone which he is holding under his arm.) Double eight double eight . . . Hello. Who's speaking? Could you please tell me . . . Hello? I'm here . . . but there's no one at the other end. I'd better dial another number. Double five double five . . . Hello? Who's speaking? Hello? This is me . . . are you there? What is the number for Information?

SIGNPOST. Try one double one!

CASPAR. (*Dialing.*) One double one! Hello, who's speaking?

SIGNPOST. Hello? Who's speaking?

CASPAR. Hello? This is me!

SIGNPOST. Hello? This is me!

CASPAR. This is Caspar.

SIGNPOST. This is the Signpost.

CASPAR. (*Dropping the phone in surprise.*) Was that you I was speaking to on the phone?

SIGNPOST. Of course. My number is one double one.

CASPAR. Do you know which way it is to Caspar's house?

SIGNPOST. Turn left and follow your nose.

CASPAR. But that's where the fog is thickest.

SIGNPOST. That's where the Giant Fog lives, by the stream. He wants you to fall in.

CASPAR. But *I* don't want to fall in.

SIGNPOST. You won't.

CASPAR. Are you sure?

SIGNPOST. Quite sure. Because Gretel has come part of the way to meet you . . . as far as the stream.

CASPAR. Why didn't she come all the way?

SIGNPOST. Because the Giant Fog stopped her.

CASPAR. She wasn't afraid to come out in the fog?

SIGNPOST. You know Gretel!

CASPAR. Then I'm not afraid to go on.

SIGNPOST. You'd better hurry or you'll be too late.

CASPAR. I'm hurrying as fast as I can. (*Exit without telephone.*)

By the stream. The Giant Fog is standing there, immovable.

GRETEL. What a thick fog! A real pea-souper!

GIANT FOG. In just the right place! By the stream!

GRETEL. Good evening, Giant Fog!

GIANT FOG. Aren't you afraid of me?

GRETEL. Well . . . I have my lantern.

GIANT FOG. That old thing! It'll go out in a moment.

GRETEL. My flashlight needed a new battery, so I could only bring the old lantern.

GIANT FOG. Pufffff! (*The light in the lantern goes out.*)

GRETEL. Oh, dear! I do hope Caspar doesn't fall in the stream now.

GIANT FOG. It'll serve him right for going out so much.

GRETEL. Most of the time he stays at home, playing with me . . . we play hide-and-seek and hopscotch or "Hello-who's-speaking?"

GIANT FOG. Really? And is Caspar always nice to you?

GRETEL. Always! Dear Giant Fog, please light my lantern again for me.

GIANT FOG. I don't have any matches—have you?

GRETEL. No. But can't you help me somehow?

GIANT FOG. (*Feeling sorry for her.*) I can't help you. But you can help yourself.

GRETEL. I'll do anything for Caspar!

GIANT FOG. You'd have to get smaller and smaller until you could climb into the lantern.

GRETEL. And then the lantern would shine again?

GIANT FOG. Yes. You'd be the light in the lantern.

GRETEL. Please, dear Giant Fog, make me smaller and smaller, so that I can climb into the lantern.

GIANT FOG. All right. First of all I'll make you half the size you are. (*He waves one of his veils.*) Abracadabra!

GRETEL. (*Disappears and returns half as big as before.* [*Gretels in two smaller sizes must be ready behind the scenes.*]) Smaller, please, dear Giant Fog.

GIANT FOG. What a brave girl you are! Next time you'll be a candle flame.

GRETEL. Will I give a good light?

GIANT FOG. As bright as the lantern gave before it went out.

GRETEL. Then please say the magic word.

GIANT FOG. Abracadabra!

GRETEL. (*Shining inside the lantern.*) Oh, how bright I am!

GIANT FOG. But you'll only be able to become Gretel again if Caspar recognizes you in the lantern.

GRETEL. I'm not afraid. My voice is still the same. And I know the magic word too.

CASPAR. (*Enters.*) Oh, there's our old lantern! It's never shone so brightly before. But where is my dear Gretel? Hello? Gretel? She must have run home because she was afraid of the Giant Fog. She's very timid, of course. Different from me! Well, at least she's left the lantern. So I'll soon be home—in time for at least ten pancakes. (*Exit.*)

At Caspar's house

CASPAR. (*Enters with lantern and puts it on the table.*) Good evening, Grandma.

GRANDMA. Isn't Gretel with you?

CASPAR. She ran away from the Giant Fog. But she left the lantern for me.

GRANDMA. Gretel hasn't come back!

GRETEL. (*Softly, from inside the lantern.*) Here I am!

CASPAR. I heard Gretel's voice.

GRANDMA. Nonsense! Where can she be?

GRETEL. Here I am!

CASPAR. That was her voice all right!

GRANDMA. It was probably your own bad conscience.

CASPAR. No, Grandma, it wasn't—it was Gretel. She must have hidden in her bedroom.

GRANDMA. Nonsense! I've been here all the time. I must go and look for her outside. (*Exit.*)

CASPAR. Call out again, Gretel. I know you're here somewhere.

GRETEL. Here I am!

CASPAR. (*Looking for her.*) Are you in *that* corner?

GRETEL. Cold!

CASPAR. *This* corner?

GRETEL. Still colder.

CASPAR. In the closet? (*He looks there.*)

GRETEL. Warmer.

CASPAR. Under the table? (*He looks there.*)

GRETEL. Much warmer.

CASPAR. Goodness! You aren't . . . (*He looks closely at the lantern.*)

GRETEL. Very warm indeed.

CASPAR. (*Delightedly.*) . . . *inside* the lantern! Dear little Gretel! (*The light goes out and Gretel [only a finger's length high] is standing beside the lantern.*) You lighted my way home! But why are you so small?

GRETEL. I couldn't have climbed into the lantern otherwise! And then I couldn't have lighted your way home.

CASPAR. But you'll get bigger again, won't you?

GRETEL. Say "Abracadabra!"

CASPAR. Abracadabra!

GRETEL. (*Disappears and returns a size bigger.*) Oh, Caspar! There's nothing you can't do. You're much cleverer than the Giant Fog.

CASPAR. I am?

GRETEL. Yes, you are! When the Giant Fog said "Abracadabra," I got smaller and smaller.

CASPAR. (*Proudly.*) And when *I* say "Abracadabra" you get bigger and bigger. Hold tight, then. Abracadabra! (*Gretel disappears and comes back in her normal size.*) Would you like me to make you even bigger?

GRETEL. No, thank you. I don't want to be bigger than you. But where is the "Hello-who's-speaking?" game?

CASPAR. We don't need that any more. The hot-and-cold game is much nicer.

GRETEL. (*Putting her arms around him.*) Dear, good Caspar!

CASPAR. Dear, good Gretel! Tomorrow I'll be sure to play with you . . . and the day after tomorrow too. But now we can enjoy our pancakes.

GRETEL. No. First of all we must find Grandma or *she*'ll fall into the stream in the fog.

CASPAR. You're quite right! And, children . . . be careful that *you* don't get lost in the fog!

GRETEL. Good-by for now, children.

Caspar and the Tollgate

Characters

CASPAR	**TOLLGATE**
GRANDMA	**MAGICIAN**
GRETEL	**BEAR**

Outside Caspar's house.

CASPAR. (*Enters, singing cheerfully.*)
    Hooray, hooray, hooray, hurrah!
    Hooray, hooray for my Grandma!
Children, we're having something extra special today—mushrooms! My Grandma has been picking mushrooms in the magic wood. (*Grandma enters with a basket.*) Dear Grandma! Did you find as many mushrooms today as yesterday?

GRANDMA. A big basketful.

CASPAR. So I can have five plates of mushrooms again today?

GRANDMA. As many as you like.

CASPAR. Can I just look at them?

GRANDMA. Look as much as you like.

CASPAR. (*Peers into the basket, then jumps back and starts croaking like a toad.*) Ugh! Ugh! Ugh!

GRANDMA. What's the matter with you? Aren't you feeling well today?

CASPAR. I'm quite well so far . . . but we won't be well if we eat your mushrooms!

GRANDMA. What's the matter with my mushrooms?

CASPAR. They're . . . they're . . . TOADSTOOLS! Didn't you notice?

GRANDMA. I'm sure they're mushrooms. I see so well with my new glasses.

CASPAR. But you aren't wearing your glasses, Grandma.

GRANDMA. (*Feeling her nose.*) Oh no! So I'm not!

CASPAR. Where are they then?

GRANDMA. That magician must have magicked them away. He was threatening to the day before yesterday.

CASPAR. And you went back in spite of that?

GRANDMA. Well . . . you're so fond of mushrooms!

CASPAR. You bet!

GRANDMA. And I'm *so* brave!

CASPAR. You bet!

GRANDMA. But I must get my glasses back.

CASPAR. I'll get them for you.

GRANDMA. You? What about the magician?

CASPAR. I'm *so* brave!

GRANDMA. You bet!

CASPAR. And *so* clever!

GRANDMA. You bet!

CASPAR. And *so* furious with that rogue of a magician!

GRANDMA. You mustn't be so furious.

CASPAR. What? No glasses! No mushrooms! Of course I'm furious.

GRANDMA. You mustn't be. I know the magician's secret. He can put a spell on anyone who's furious.

CASPAR. What sort of a spell?

GRANDMA. Whatever sort he wants.

CASPAR. Then I'd better not be furious when I meet him.

GRANDMA. That's better. Be polite to the magician. Say, "Please, Mr. Magician," and "After you, Mr. Magician." And bow to him, like this. (*She gives a little bow.*) Then perhaps he'll give you back my glasses.

CASPAR. Oh, well . . . I'll be polite to the magician. I'll say, "Please, Mr. Magician." "After you, Mr. Magician." And I'll bow to him, like this . . . (*He gives a little bow.*)

GRANDMA. That's right. And now I must go and get our lunch. Steak and mashed potatoes, without mushrooms! (*Exit.*)

CASPAR. Without mushrooms! I'll make that ragamuffin of a magician pay for this! (*Starts to run off.*)

GRETEL. (*Enters and stops him.*) Where are you going, Caspar?

CASPAR. I'm going to see that rogue of a ruffian of a magician who's stolen our Grandma's glasses in the magic wood so that we can't have mushrooms for lunch! (*Takes a deep breath.*) If he doesn't give me the glasses and a big basket of mushrooms as well . . .

GRETEL. I'm not going to let you go, Caspar!

CASPAR. Who's going to get Grandma's glasses, then?

GRETEL. *I* will.

CASPAR. (*Laughing at her.*) You? Dear Gretel, you'd be afraid of a fly! And you know very well you're afraid of the magician.

GRETEL. Yes, I'm very afraid of him.

CASPAR. *I'm* not afraid. I'm *so* brave! And *so* clever!

GRETEL. And *so* furious!

CASPAR. Yes! I'm exploding with fury!

GRETEL. But you know, don't you, that the magician can cast a spell on anyone who's furious? So it's much better if I go instead of you.

CASPAR. No. You must stay at home with Grandma, and be a good little girl. Get along with you . . . to the kitchen! (*Exit Gretel.*)

CASPAR. (*To himself.*) And Caspar must go to find the magician. Get along with you, Caspar . . . to the magic wood!

At the edge of the magic wood. The entrance is barred by a tollgate, which can be lifted and let down by means of a wire.

CASPAR. (*Enters with a large pair of scissors. He doesn't notice the tollgate because he starts talking immediately, turning toward the children.*) Now, children, here I am at the edge of the magic wood. (*Flies into a rage.*) That rascally rapscallion of a magician! I'll teach him a thing or two! Children, do you happen to know the magician's name?

CHILDREN. No.

CASPAR. Then listen carefully. His name is Kakukikikukakorum. Can you remember all that?

CHILDREN. Yes (and no).

CASPAR. Let's try to say it together. One! Two! Three!

CHILDREN. (*They try to say the name.*)

CASPAR. That wasn't quite right. But it's the magician's fault for having such a long name. Luckily I've brought my scissors with me. So we can just cut a bit off his long, long name. We'll do that together, shall we? I'll say the name very slowly, and you say "Now!" when I'm to cut a bit off. Now then, Ka-ku . . .

CHILDREN. Now!

CASPAR. (*Snips with the scissors.* [*The handle can be tied to a nail in the playboard, or the scissors can simply lie on top of the playboard.*]) There! Now the magician's name is just Kikikukakorum. Let's say that all together. (*Children can't get it quite right yet.*)

CASPAR. That's still not quite right. We must cut a bit more off. Say "Now!" again, when you want me to cut. Come on! Ki-ki . . .

CHILDREN. Now!

CASPAR. (*Snips again with the scissors.*) There! Now he's called Kuka-korum! That's quite enough, isn't it! (*He beats time with the scissors.*) Ku-ka-ko-rum!

CHILDREN. Ku-ka-ko-rum!

CASPAR. Well done, children! I'm glad we've cut the magician's name down to size. Do you feel as furious with him as I do?

CHILDREN. Yes!

CASPAR. It's all right for you. You don't have to be polite to him. You don't have to say, "Please, Mr. Magician," and "After you, Mr. Magician." And you don't have to bow to him, like this . . . (*He bows, and hits his head on the tollgate. As he does so, he drops the scissors.*) Ow! What's this silly thing? I've never seen anything like it before. Hey! You! Are you a fallen flagpole?

TOLLGATE. No.

CASPAR. Were you once a ship's mast?

TOLLGATE. No.

CASPAR. You must be a no-pole then.

TOLLGATE. I happen to be a tollgate. I mark boundaries. You can find me all over the place. You can't go any farther unless I let you.

CASPAR. Well, I want to go farther now, so you'd better let me.

TOLLGATE. I don't feel so inclined, I'm afraid.

CASPAR. I'll get you out of my way. (*He tries to lift the tollgate.*) Heave-ho! Heave-ho! (*He surveys the results.*) You've gone up a little, but I must do better than that. Will you help me, children?

CHILDREN. (*Shout with Caspar.*) Heave-ho! Heave-ho! (*At last the tollgate is standing upright.*)

CASPAR. There we are. Now I know where this stupid no-pole has come from. The magician magicked it here to guard the wood. But he can't stop Caspar!

TOLLGATE. Yes, he can! (*The tollgate hits Caspar over the head.*)

CASPAR. Ow! Ow! I stopped that one all right!

MAGICIAN. (*Appearing behind the tollgate.*) Right!

CASPAR. (*Recovering himself.*) Please, Mr. Magician . . .

MAGICIAN. Caspar is the stupidest boy I've ever met!

CASPAR. After you, Mr. Magician.

MAGICIAN. Impudent, too.

CASPAR. Not at all, Mr. Magician. I'm very polite, like my Grandma likes me to be.

MAGICIAN. Don't talk to me about your Grandma.

CASPAR. Mr. Magician, how long have you been wearing glasses?

MAGICIAN. Are you hinting at something?

CASPAR. Yes, I am! You've stolen them! (*Working himself up into a rage again.*) You nasty thieving, Grandma-grieving ruffian!

MAGICIAN. How dare you! (*He lifts one hand and the tollgate hits Caspar over the head again.*)

CASPAR. (*Scrambling to his feet.*) I'll snatch those glasses off your ugly, bright red nose, you Kukakorum, you! Ooh, I'm furious! Simply furious!

MAGICIAN. (*Lifts his hand again and the tollgate hits Caspar over the head a third time. The lights go out and there is a clap of thunder. Then Caspar reappears as a bear, but the bear is wearing his pointed Caspar cap, which is impervious to spells. The bear has a chain around his neck and the magician ties it to the tollgate.*) Ha ha ha! So much for all your fury! You're a Bruin bear! With a sore head! And I'm going to keep your Grandma's glasses. And you can keep your chain. You'll never be Caspar again unless the chain breaks. And it'll never break if I know anything about chains. (*He tests the chain's strength.*) Heave-ho! Heave-ho! Not a chance! Caspar will have to go on being a bear. With a Caspar cap!

GRETEL. (*Comes running up, sees the bear and shrinks back.*) Oh, goodness! What's that?

MAGICIAN. That's Bruin, my bear!

GRETEL. Does he bite?

MAGICIAN. You bet!

GRETEL. Then I think I won't go too close to him.

MAGICIAN. No. Better not.

GRETEL. You must be the Lord High Master Kakukikikukakorum.

MAGICIAN. (*Flattered.*) How nicely you pronounce my name!

GRETEL. How handsome you look, Mr. Magician. But it's a shame you

have to wear glasses—they make you look older than your age.

MAGICIAN. Is that better? (*He takes off the glasses.*)

GRETEL. Much better. How long have you had your bear?

MAGICIAN. (*Hesitates.*) Er . . . oh, quite some time.

GRETEL. I've never seen him here before. Nor that pole.

MAGICIAN. Careful! That's a tollgate. But why have you come to see me, anyway?

GRETEL. In the first place, because you have such a lovely wood.

MAGICIAN. And in the second place?

GRETEL. Because you're the cleverest magician in the world. At least, that's what I've heard.

MAGICIAN. Yes, I am!

GRETEL. So you could turn me into whatever you wanted?

MAGICIAN. Only if you were in a furious temper.

GRETEL. (*Cautiously.*) Well, I'm not. But I would have thought the cleverest magician in the world could cast a spell on anyone without their having to be in a furious temper.

MAGICIAN. But in that case I could only turn you into something you *wanted* to be turned into. And I'd have to turn you back into yourself when you asked me.

GRETEL. That's all right.

MAGICIAN. I'd have to go and get my book of spells.

GRETEL. Oh, do please get it, Lord High Magician Kakukikikukakorum.

MAGICIAN. Well, all right . . . but it's only because you say my name so nicely! (*Exit.*)

GRETEL. (*After the magician has gone.*) Now you must help me quickly, children! Is Bruin a real bear?

CHILDREN. No.

GRETEL. Then he must be Caspar.

CHILDREN. Yes.

GRETEL. I guessed that because of his Caspar cap! The magician was able to put a spell on him because he was furious, wasn't he?

CHILDREN. Yes.

GRETEL. If Bruin is really Caspar it's quite safe for me to go up to him . . . (*She does that.*) . . . and stroke him . . . (*She does that.*) . . . and ask him what I can do to get him changed back. Please, Caspar, whisper in my ear. (*She bends down to listen.*) Oh, he says someone must break his chain. Is that right, children?

CHILDREN. Yes.

GRETEL. I wonder if I'm strong enough. (*She tries to break the chain.*) Oh, dear! I'm *not* strong enough. What shall I do? But I have an idea! There's only one solution. You must get furious again, Caspar! (*Bruin growls.*) I'll have to make you very angry. (*Bruin growls more angrily.*) If you burst with rage, perhaps you'll burst your bonds too! (*Bruin growls very angrily indeed.*) Quiet, now . . . Kukakorum's coming back with his book of spells.

MAGICIAN. (*Enters with his book.*) Now I must put my glasses on again, or I won't be able to find the right one.

GRETEL. Yes, they suit you very well for reading.

MAGICIAN. Now, then, what shall I turn you into?

GRETEL. Into a . . . (*She hesitates.*) . . . a fly.

MAGICIAN. A common or garden fly?

GRETEL. No. A bluebottle, please. The kind that buzzes very loudly.

MAGICIAN. That's easy. Just a second! (*He leafs through his book of spells.*) Yes. Here we are!
    Bluebottle, bluebottle, buzzing by,
    Gretel's a girl—or is she a fly?

(*The lights go out and there is a clap of thunder. Gretel disappears and there is a buzzing sound. The magician and Bruin follow the imaginary fly with their eyes.*) What does that stupid fly want? (*Bruin growls and tries to swat the fly dancing in front of his nose.*) Quiet now, Bruin! (*Bruin growls more angrily and takes a swipe at the fly.*) Go on! Go on! Make him furious! (*Bruin growls very loudly and jumps about so violently that the chain breaks. The lights go out again and after another thunderclap Caspar is seen standing in Bruin's place.*)

CASPAR. You see, Mr. Kukakorum!

MAGICIAN. None of your impudence, you . . . (*As he speaks, the fly—now visible—buzzes around his nose. [Behind the scenes three flies in three different sizes must be ready on stiff wires.]*) Leave me alone! (*Two larger flies buzz around him and he tries to swat them.*) I can see I'll have to change you back, young Gretel, if you're going to bring other flies into my wood. (*The flies circle around him in larger circles. He opens his book of spells again.*)
    Bluebottle, bluebottle, buzzing by,
    You are Gretel, not a fly.

(*The lights go out and there is a clap of thunder. Gretel appears again in front of the magician, snatches his glasses and darts away while he gropes nearsightedly after her.*)

GRETEL. You see, Mr. Kukakorum! Or, rather, you *don't* see!

MAGICIAN. Where are you, you two rascals? And where are my glasses?

GRETEL. *Grandma's* glasses, you mean old thing! They hopped off your nose when they heard the thunderclap.

MAGICIAN. And where's that impudent rascal, Caspar?

CASPAR. (*Off stage.*) Here! (*The tollgate hits the magician over the head so that he falls to the ground. He lies there motionless. Caspar comes up to him.*) We've won, Gretel!

GRETEL. Oh, Caspar, I'm so glad you aren't a bear any longer.

CASPAR. Oh, Gretel, I'm so glad you aren't a bluebottle any longer.

GRETEL. I was so afraid you might hurt me with your claws.

CASPAR. But you were *so* brave! And *so* clever!

GRETEL. And *so* furious with that old magician!

CASPAR. But he didn't know you were furious.

GRETEL. How dared he wear Grandma's glasses!

CASPAR. We must give them back to her.

GRETEL. So that she can go out picking mushrooms tomorrow morning.

CASPAR. And we'll use the tollgate for firewood! (*He takes the tollgate under one arm and prods the magician with his foot.*) Come along, Mr. Magician! Wake up! And don't lose your way in your wood now that you haven't any glasses. And say, "After you," politely, tomorrow morning early when we're picking mushrooms!

MAGICIAN. (*Standing up and groaning.*) Oh, dear . . . I feel like a bear with a sore head. I don't feel at all well! I think I must have eaten too many mushrooms.

CASPAR. Get well soon, Mr. Magician.

MAGICIAN. Oh, dear! Oh, dear! (*Exit.*)

CASPAR. Good-by, Mr. Magician. And, children, be careful when you're picking mushrooms, won't you! Do you know the difference between mushrooms and toadstools?

CHILDREN. Yes (and no).

CASPAR. Well, as I say, you must be careful. There are a lot of rascally, mock-mushrooms around, and it's no joke if you make a mistake. But now we must go home. Grandma needs her glasses. And we mustn't keep Grandma waiting, must we? So good-by for now, children.

Notes for Puppeteers

We gratefully acknowledge the help of Kitty Lutz, Assistant Storytelling and Group Work Specialist, New York Public Library, in preparing the Notes and Bibliography for the American edition.

STAGE

The main purpose of the puppet stage is to provide a background for the puppets and to hide the puppeteer. There are many kinds of stages you can make for a puppet show. Some are quite elaborate but you can make a simple one for yourself either indoors or out. Remember that the stage should be high enough for the puppeteer to stand without the top of his head showing. Some stages are made so that the puppeteer can sit down, but it is better to stand in order to get more movement from the puppets. Other stages are collapsible so that they can be stored and carried easily.

Outdoors you can use a clothesline or tie a line between two trees and hang a rug or a sheet or bedspread over it. Any large piece of cloth will do. Indoors a line across a doorway will serve the same purpose. A large box or a table on top of another table can also be used. In this case the table should be covered with cloth to conceal the puppeteer. Materials you can find at home or at school will be useful. At school, the blackboard will make a good background on which to draw the scenery. At home, plain wall behind the stage can serve as the backdrop for the puppets.

SCENERY

If you use a plain background, signs saying, for example, "Grandmother's House" or "Forest Ranger's House" can be made to tell the audience where the play is taking place, or Caspar can tell the audience himself. These methods work well if there are several scenes in one play as the scenery will not have to be changed during the play. You may wish to have different colored backgrounds, such as green for the forest scenes or black for night. Painted scenery also works very well. You may wish to draw the scenery on a large piece of paper and hang it on the wall behind the stage. Use masking tape to hang the scenery as it will not damage the walls. Remember that the scenery does not need to be fancy or perfectly drawn. A house and a tree or two are all that is necessary. Keep the scenery simple because the puppets are the important part of the play.

LIGHTING

A lamp or a large flashlight at the sides of the stage will be sufficient for lighting. Side lighting is more effective than front lighting, but it is not essential.

More elaborate stages have curtains and detailed scenery. These, too, are fun to make but require more work and materials. There are many books on the making of puppets that will be useful to you here, and some of these are listed at the end of this book.

PUPPETS

Now what about Caspar and the other puppets you need? You can buy puppets but often you will have more fun and satisfaction if you make them yourself. There are many kinds of puppets and many ways to make them. The ones we will talk about here are hand puppets rather than rod or string puppets.

Hand puppets consist of a head, which can be made of many kinds of material, and a body, which is usually made of cloth. The head is hollow so that you can put one finger in it and a finger in each of the sleeves to bring the puppet to life. Some people prefer using their first finger for the head and the thumb and middle finger for the hands. Others use the first, or the first and middle fingers, for the head and the little finger and thumb for the hands. You should practice to develop a method which feels right to you and with which you can make the puppet move the best.

Puppets can be made of almost anything—paper bags, boxes, cloth, plastic bottles, even vegetables. Traditionally Caspar puppets have wooden heads, but you will probably find it easier to make simpler ones first unless you are very good at carving. Clay and papier-mâché are the most fun to work with because with them you can make the head exactly as you picture it.

The head is modeled first in clay. A plastic base clay is good because it does not dry out and can be used over and over again. After the head is modeled, soak strips of paper in a paste of flour and water and put them over the head in layers. You will need to make several layers of papier-mâché. An easy way to do this is to use regular newspaper for the first layer, comic sections for the second, and then alternate the two for the remaining layers. Be sure to mold the features you had on the original clay model, and be sure to leave an opening in the neck for your finger. When the papier-mâché is dry, cut the head open and take out the clay. Then you are ready to paste your puppet head back together with more papier-mâché and to paint it. Balloons are also a good base for the head. Although you will have to mold the features of your puppet with the papier-mâché, you will not have to cut open the head when the mâché is dry. Just puncture the balloon with a pin and pull it out.

It does not matter about the size of the puppet heads. They should be large enough to be seen by everyone in your audience, and the characters in each play should be about the same size. Four to six inches is a good size for the heads.

PAINTING
Puppets can be painted with poster paints but these have a tendency to crack as they get older. Acrilic paints are very good.

COSTUMES
Now you are ready to dress your puppets. Remember that they will have to fit over the hand of the puppeteer and that the sleeves should be big

enough for the puppeteer's fingers. Costumes can be made of old bits of cloth. You can use your imagination here. Don't forget Caspar's cap! Some Caspar puppets have legs, but these are not usual in hand puppets. The costumes should be long enough to cover most of the forearm. Hair can be painted on, or it may be made of yarn or paper curls and glued to the puppet's head.

PERFORMANCE

The figures must come on from the side, except for devils, witches and other such characters, who should rise up from beneath the playboard. No figure should ever hide another, just as in a stage play. Remember to hold your arms well up and never let the puppets sink below the playboard.

Figures must look at the puppet they are talking to. If the puppet is talking to the audience, he should look at them. Only the puppet which is speaking should move, otherwise it is hard to tell which puppet is talking when they don't have moving mouths. Words and movements should always match each other. The movements will look natural if they are deliberate and economical. There should be a reason for every move. Try to think as the puppet would and move accordingly. If your puppet is picking up anything, be sure to grasp it firmly. Practice walking so that the puppet will look realistic.

The person who is moving the puppet should also speak his lines. The play should be written down and taped inside the playboard so that it can be read. It is better to memorize the play because then you are free to concentrate on the puppet's movement. If you have a tape recorder, you may want to experiment with that. Some puppeteers put their plays on tape and move the puppets to the taped words. You should try not to put on a play which is too difficult for your audience, though even this is better than a coy one which talks down to them.

The front rows of the audience shouldn't be too close to the theater. It is a good idea to sit in the first row after you set up the stage, to see if the puppets are visible.

Audience participation is fun in a puppet show. You will notice that in several of the Caspar plays Caspar speaks right to the audience. The audience will always answer—so don't let things get out of hand. If the audience begins to interrupt the dialogue, take the puppets off the stage for a few moments.

When the audience is a small one, Caspar can get to know all the children, and there are a hundred different ways he can begin talking to them. At school, he can talk about arithmetic or some other school subject to break the ice. He can persuade tongue-tied children to talk, he can teach road safety. But he should never spoil well-loved stories. It is easy to do this, for instance, if fairy tales are turned into plays for Caspar shows. So why not think up new plays which are full of surprises? The basic rule is that every play must have a happy ending, the good must triumph and the bad be overcome.

Try to think up little scenes for yourself. Remember, you have to believe in your puppets and an easy way to get to know them is the way to get to know anybody—talk to them. Get in conversation with the puppets. Ask the policeman what he's doing today. Talk to Grandma about her shopping and to Caspar's uncle—the forest ranger—about a forest fire. Rehearse first without an audience, and then to a few critical friends. There are innumerable situations which can be used as plots for puppet plays. Let Grandma look all over the house for her glasses and discover finally, when she's in front of the mirror, that they've been on her nose all the time! Let Caspar meet Mr. Too-Clever-By-Half waiting at the bus stop. Use short scenes from everyday life—this is all that the traditional puppeteers had as their material when they played in the old days to passers-by in the streets and their audience often had time to watch only one or two short scenes.

Caspar is a children's hero, like Robin Hood or Jack the Giant-Killer or Peter Pan. And he is an individual just as they are. He knows everyone—from devils and giants to kings and queens. He makes mistakes and is sometimes foolish, but in his fights against the wicked he is clever and courageous and good.

Of the ten plays in this book, seven need three or four hands and three can be put on with only two hands—that is, by a single puppeteer. Other people can, of course, help by handing objects to the puppeteer behind the scenes. In the last play, for instance, they could hand the three different flies on three stiff wires.

You can get at least as much fun from thinking out ways of keeping the show lively as from the actual operation of the puppets. You don't need to stick to the script—everyone should feel free to alter it as he wishes. The main thing is that the puppets should be lively. There need be no limit to the puppeteer's bright ideas!

A Bibliography of Puppet Books

FOR BEGINNERS

* Ackley, Edith Flack. *Marionettes*. Illus. by Marjorie Flack. Philadelphia: J. B. Lippincott Co., 1929. Directions for making simple cloth string puppets plus five puppet plays.

Cummings, Richard. *101 Hand Puppets*. Illus. by the author. New York: David McKay Co., Inc., 1962. Directions for easy puppets using a variety of materials.

Jagendorf, Moritz. *Puppets for Beginners*. Illus. by Jean Michenor. Boston: Plays, Inc., 1966. A simple and colorfully illustrated craft book for the youngest puppeteer.

Lewis, Shari. *Making Easy Puppets*. Illus. by Larry Lurin. New York: E. P. Dutton & Co., Inc., 1967. Clever ideas for making figures from vegetables and boxes as well as for hand puppets.

* Pels, Gertrude. *Easy Puppets*. Illus. by Albert Pels. New York: Thomas Y. Crowell Company, 1951. Easy-to-follow instructions with large print and clear diagrams for making hand puppets from various materials.

* Snook, Barbara. *Puppets*. Newton Centre, Mass.: Charles T. Branford Co., 1966. Clear directions and diagrams for older children or teachers and parents.

ADVANCED AND ADULT

* Batchelder, Marjorie. *Puppet Theatre Handbook*. Illus. by Douglas Anderson. New York: Harper & Row, Publishers, 1947. An advanced and complete book of instructions for all phases of puppetry, including its philosophy and the construction of puppets, costumes, stage and production.

* Indicates especially recommended titles.

* Ficklen, Bessie Alexander. *A Handbook of Fist Puppets.* Illus. by Julie Brown. Philadelphia: J. B. Lippincott Co., 1935. Very good and detailed instructions for making a variety of types of hand puppets, with information on their handling and on production of the plays. Includes three plays as well as a few short sketches.

* Inverarity, R. B. *A Manual of Puppetry.* Portland, Oreg.: Binfords & Mort, 1938. Construction of marionettes and other puppets with a detailed section on manipulation and production.

Morton, Brenda. *Needlework Puppets.* Illus. by Irene Haskins. Boston: Plays, Inc. Instructions for simple cloth hand puppets which require some sewing ability.

Mulholland, John. *Practical Puppetry.* Illus. by Jack Parker. New York: Arco Publishing Co., Inc., 1962. A good manual for the puppeteer on the construction of stages and hand, rod, shadow and string puppets.

HISTORY

* Baird, Bil. *The Art of the Puppet.* New York: The Macmillan Company, 1965. A well-illustrated history of puppetry from earliest times by a famous puppeteer. For adults.

von Boehn, Max. *Dolls and Puppets.* New York: Cooper Square Publishers, Inc., 1967. A complete and scholarly reference book on the history of dolls and puppets. For the student of the subject.

Philpot, A. R. *Let's Look at Puppets.* Illus. by Norma Burgin. Chicago: Albert Whitman & Co., 1966. A short history of puppetry for children which covers countries all over the world.

Speaight, George. *The History of the English Puppet Theatre.* Boston: Plays, Inc., 1955. The development and origins of the English puppet theater. For adults and older children.

FOR TEACHERS

Binyon, Helen. *Puppetry Today.* New York: Watson-Guptill Publications, 1966. Directions for string, hand and rod puppets with some history of puppetry by a puppeteer who works with adults.

Bodor, John. *Creating and Presenting Hand Puppets.* Illus. with photographs. New York: Reinhold Publishing Corp., 1967. A detailed book which lists the materials needed, steps to follow and classroom time needed for each project.

Howard, Vernon. *Puppet and Pantomime Plays.* Illus. by Doug Anderson. New

York: Sterling Publishing Co., Inc., 1962. Emphasis on the creative approach to puppetry, giving suggestions for puppets and for plots but leaving the actual words to the performer.

* *Indicates especially recommended titles.*

j832 Baumann, Hans, 1914-
B327c   Caspar and his friends; a
         collection of puppet plays.
         Illus. by Richard Lebenson.
400   by Joyce Emerson. Walck, 19

INV. 78

Free Public Library.
NEW HAVEN, CONN.